Adventures of a Toddler

Jack Do It!

The Playground

CHARLES BAUER

PAGE PUBLISHING
Conneaut Lake, PA

First originally published by Page Publishing 2022

ISBN 979-8-88654-215-8 (pbk)
ISBN 979-8-88654-216-5 (digital)

Printed in the United States of America

To my grandson Jack Bauer whose boundless energy provides so much entertainment and unforgettable memories. Your love of play, your contagious smile, and your laugh constantly reminds us to enjoy every moment of this life and be the best version of ourselves. All my love, Grandpa.

Once upon a time, there was a very active toddler boy named Jack. Soon after, Jack learned how to walk; he never slowed down. Jack loved to run everywhere. He had boundless energy. On the playground, Jack's parents were always there to make sure he wouldn't get hurt.

However, when Jack turned two, he discovered something about himself.

One Saturday morning, when Jack's parents took Jack to the playground, he ran off and jumped up onto the climbing bars. His momma panicked and ran over to help Jack.

Jack held out his hand and said, "Momma, Jack do it!"

He walked the entire length of the climbing bars and hopped off with a big smile. Jack's momma had a tear in her eye.

8

Jack was so proud of his accomplishment that he ran over to the big slide. Jack's dad followed him with a concerned look. Jack began to climb the ladder to the big slide, and as his dad was standing behind him, he turned and said, "Dada, Jack do it!"

Jack reached the top of the ladder and, without hesitation, slid down the slide, where his dad was waiting to catch him.

Jack smiled at his dad and jumped to his feet and ran off to the climbing wall.

Jack's parents looked at each other and shrugged their shoulders. They both walked to the climbing wall, and Momma asked, "Jack, if you need help, just ask me or Dad, okay?"

Jack said, "Jack do it!" and proceeded to very carefully climb up the wall, watching while he placed each foot where he could maintain his balance.

Once Jack made it to the top, he realized he was unsure how to get down. So he yelled, "Dada, catch me!" and he quickly jumped into his dad's arms.

Jack immediately said, "Down, Dada," and he ran off to the swings. He stood by the swings and was seen staring at the swings very intently, wondering how he would get on the swing.

There were already two children on the swings with their parents pushing them. But there was one swing open.

Jack's parents walked over to the swings, and Momma asked, "Jack, are you okay?"

Jack responded in a soft voice, "Momma, help me?"

Momma placed Jack on the swing, and his dad pushed him from behind.

20

As Jack's dad was pushing Jack higher and higher, he began to scream, "Weeee!" and the other two kids did the same. Jack's parents were all smiles.

As they were getting ready to leave the playground, Jack didn't want to go back into his stroller for the journey home. He looked up at his mom and dad and asked, "Hand, Dada and Momma?"

Jack's dad responded, "If you are going to walk, you must always hold hands!"

As they walked home hand in hand, Jack proclaimed one last time, "Jack do it!" and looked up at his parents with a huge smile.

About the Author

Charles Bauer retired as a teacher as well as a soccer and golf coach in June 2020. He began his teaching career in 1976 at Staten Island Academy, where he taught fifth and sixth-grade history and coached soccer and softball for seven years. He obtained his MBA and worked in the banking industry for over twenty years, during which time he served as a disaster recovery professional during 9/11. He returned to teaching in 2008 in the Commack School District, where he taught history and coached soccer and golf. During his tenure in the Commack School District he obtained his second Masters degree in Educational Administration and Leadership.

Always looking for new ways to recreate and bring history to life for his students, Charles created a connection through Skype with both students from Afghanistan and Japan so that his students could view history through a unique lens. Additionally, his classes were also frequent visitors to the 9/11 Museum and the Long Island Slavery Museum. Since retiring in 2020, Charles has become very involved in kayaking, hiking, and biking and created his own website www.theriverchaz.com, as well as an Instagram account, @theriverchaz, which provides reviews of kayaking, hiking, and biking opportunities throughout the United States, as well as globally.

Lightning Source UK Ltd.
Milton Keynes UK
UKHW052256030123
414767UK00005B/59